Madam C. J. Walker

Building a Business Empire

MADAM C.J. WALKER

by Penny Colman

A Gateway Biography
The Millbrook Press
Brookfield, Connecticut

*For Hedy Leutner, another woman who
works hard, helps people, and enjoys life.*

*Special thanks to Wilma L. Gibbs and
Susan Sutton, staff members at the
Indiana Historical Society.*

*Also special thanks to the staff at
the Madame Walker Urban Life Center,
including Josephine Weathers-Rogers,
Cheryl Coleman, and Serena Hopkinson.*

Library of Congress Cataloging-in-Publication Data

Colman, Penny.
Madam C. J. Walker/by Penny Colman.
p.   cm.—(A Gateway biography)
Includes bibliographical references and index.
Summary: A biography of the businesswoman who was born in poverty
on a Louisiana plantation, founded her own hair care business, and
made more money than any woman, black or white, had ever made
in America.
ISBN 1-56294-338-3
1. Walker, C. J., Madam, 1867-1919—Juvenile literature.   2. Afro-
American women executives—Biography—Juvenile literature.
3. Cosmetics industry—United States—History—Juvenile literature.
[1. Walker, C. J., Madam, 1867-1919.   2. Businesswomen.   3. Afro-
Americans—Biography.   4. Cosmetics industry—History.]   I. Title.
II. Series.
HD9970.5C672W354   1994
338.7'66855'092—dc20   [B]   93-13824   CIP   AC

Cover photograph courtesy of Madam C. J. Walker Collection,
Indiana Historical Society Library

Photographs all courtesy of Madam C. J. Walker Collection,
Indiana Historical Society Library, except The Metropolitan
Museum of Art, Morris K. Jesup Fund, 1940: p. 11; Library of
Congress: p. 39; Penny Colman: p. 43

Photo research by Penny Colman

Published by The Millbrook Press
2 Old New Milford Road, Brookfield, Connecticut 06804

Madam C. J. Walker

*Madam C. J. Walker. She was fond of elegant dresses,
like the one she wears in this photo.*

Madam C. J. Walker made lots of money. More money than probably any woman—black or white —had ever made before in America. And Madam Walker made the money herself. She started her own business and built a factory.

Walker revolutionized the business of developing and selling hair-care products for black women. She did it during the early 1900s, when life for blacks was hard and sometimes very dangerous. Mobs of white people killed, or lynched, black people, segregation (the separation of groups of people according to race) was legal, and women did not have the same rights as men, including the right to vote.

Madam Walker did much more than make a lot of money. Her hair-care products helped women have a better sense of their own beauty. Walker's business also gave work to many black women. And she helped other people, especially black artists and civil rights causes, by giving wholeheartedly of her money and her time.

"My object in life is not simply to make money for myself or to spend it on myself," she said. "I love to use a part of what I make in trying to help others." Madam C. J. Walker never forgot where she came from or stopped dreaming of how life could be.

For most of her life, Madam Walker had very little money. She was born Sarah Breedlove on December 23, 1867, in a cabin on a cotton plantation owned by Robert W. Burney in Delta, Louisiana. Burney's plantation covered acres of dark-brown soil that stretched along the Mississippi River.

The Breedloves' cabin had just one room, with a fireplace at one end, a few windows without glass panes, and a front porch that ran the length of the house. The sides of the cabin were bare boards with cracks between them, and when it rained, the roof leaked.

Until the Civil War ended in 1865, two years before Sarah was born, her parents, Owen and Minerva, her brother Alex, and sister Louvenia were slaves on Burney's plantation. After the Union Army won the war, the Breedloves and all the other slaves in America were free, but life was still hard.

Many white people refused to hire free black people. Banks would not lend them money so that they could buy land or a house. Former slaves were kept from learning how to do jobs other than farm work or manual labor. Many white Southerners joined secret racist organizations such as the Ku Klux Klan. They terrorized black people by destroying their property, whipping them, and lynching them. Despite these obstacles, black people worked hard to build new lives as free people.

The Breedloves decided to stay at Burney's plantation, only now they were sharecroppers instead of slaves. They stayed in their cabin and did the same work growing cotton. Now they could sell the cotton they grew to earn money. The problem was that first the Breedloves had to "share" part of their crop with Burney. He could decide how big his share would be, and he usually took a big one. Even when the cotton crop was good, the Breedloves did not make much money. When bad weather or insects damaged the crop, they ended up owing money to Burney.

The Breedloves worked long hours planting, weeding, and picking cotton. By age five, Sarah was working in the field with her family. The sun was very hot, the ground was hard, and the air was dusty. The boll, or pod, that the white fluffy cotton came from was rough and hurt Sarah's fingers.

Sarah also helped her mother and Louvenia when they washed clothes for their family or took in white people's laundry to earn money. There were no washing machines or running water. The water from the Mississippi was too muddy to use, so clean water for washing came from cisterns, or tanks, where rainwater collected.

Sarah helped her mother and sister carry buckets of water to fill big wooden washtubs. They heated the water over the fire. Then, after sorting the laundry, scrubbing it on washboards, rinsing it with plain water, and wringing it out, they hung each piece on a line to dry. The wet laundry was heavy, and the soap had lye in it, a strong substance that got laundry clean but hurt people's skin. After a day of washing, Sarah and her mother and sister had red, cracked, sore hands and tired, aching arms and backs. The year Sarah turned seven, life got even harder. In 1874 her mother and father died of yellow fever, a disease carried by mosquitoes. In

This painting, "The Way They Live," by Thomas Anshutz, shows black sharecroppers in the late 1800s. The Breedloves endured the hard life of sharecropping at this time.

11

those days there was no vaccine against yellow fever, and thousands of people died in epidemics, sudden outbreaks of the disease that spread fast.

Sarah, Louvenia, and Alex tried to stay together. They worked very hard, but before long, Alex left. Boarding a ferry, he crossed the Mississippi River to go to the big city of Vicksburg, Mississippi, with the hope of finding a job. When he could not find work there, he headed west. Eventually, he settled in Denver, Colorado.

By washing even more clothes for white people, Louvenia and Sarah managed to stay in their cabin for a few years more. But in 1878 they grew desperate and decided to move to Vicksburg too.

Sarah and Louvenia were able to support themselves in Vicksburg as washerwomen. Then Louvenia married a man named Willie Powell, and Sarah lived with them. But Willie was a cruel man, and life was almost too hard for Sarah to bear. When she was fourteen years old, she decided to marry Moses (Jeff) McWilliams. Years later Sarah recalled that she married McWilliams "to get a home of my own." Three years later, in 1885, Sarah and Jeff had a baby daughter. They named her Lelia.

Jeff McWilliams worked at any job he could find. He loaded and unloaded steamboats, hauled heavy items, worked on building crews for the railroad, and did chores on nearby farms. Sarah McWilliams washed clothes and took care of Lelia. "If I have accomplished anything in life, it is because I have been willing to work hard," she said many years later.

Within two years of Lelia's birth, Jeff McWilliams was killed—perhaps in a race riot—in Greenwood, Mississippi, where he had gone to look for work. Alone with her baby, Sarah McWilliams was determined to make it on her own. "I never yet started anything doubtingly," she said, "and I have always believed in keeping at things with a vim [a burst of energy]."

With that attitude, Sarah McWilliams decided to move to St. Louis, Missouri. She had heard that washerwomen made more money there. She also got the names of people in St. Louis who rented rooms to boarders. So, in 1887, Sarah and Lelia

McWilliams boarded a steamboat and traveled north up the Mississippi River to St. Louis.

Built along the banks of the Mississippi, St. Louis was the third largest city in the United States at the time. During the Civil War, St. Louis had been the western headquarters for the Union Army. When McWilliams arrived, it was the headquarters for a long list of businesses—breweries, tobacco factories, railroad companies, and drug and cosmetic companies. Thousands of black people had moved to St. Louis to find jobs in the factories. They also came to escape the discrimination and violence they had faced in southern states.

Blacks had always been treated poorly in the South. But things had gotten worse since Reconstruction, the period after the Civil War when the federal government tried to protect the rights of black people. Reconstruction officially ended in 1877 when President Rutherford B. Hayes withdrew the last federal troops from southern states. Now even more black people were being beaten or lynched by white mobs. And southern states started passing laws that made it difficult for black people to vote. Other laws, known as Jim Crow laws, were passed to keep black people and white people apart. Blacks were forced to go to separate schools, ride in the back of streetcars, live in separate neighborhoods, drink from separate water fountains, and stay out of parks for "whites only."

Although there was some violence and discrimination in St. Louis, black people had a chance to live a better and safer life, and Sarah McWilliams was determined to do just that. Years later, she spoke at a meeting of black women and remembered, "I had little or no opportunity when I started out in life, having been left an orphan. . . . I had to make my own living and my own opportunity! But I made it! That is why I want to say to every Negro woman present, don't sit down and wait for the opportunity to come. . . . Get up and make them!"

Mc*Williams worked* all day washing clothes, and she attended public school at night to get the education she had missed as a child. She also made sure that her daughter went to school. By the time Lelia graduated from high school, McWilliams had managed to save enough money to send her to Knoxville College in Tennessee. For a time, Sarah McWilliams was married to a man named John Davis, but then she divorced him.

Shortly after she arrived in St. Louis, McWilliams joined the St. Paul African Methodist Episcopal Church, and its members were very kind and helpful to her and Lelia. McWilliams tried to help people, too, even though she did not have much money. She shared what she had and asked wealthy people to donate money, food, and clothing to the poor. McWilliams never forgot one of her favorite prayers:

> *Lord, help me live from day to day*
> *In such a self-forgetful way*
> *That when I ever kneel to pray*
> *My prayers shall be for others.*

Sarah McWilliams learned a lot in St. Louis. She also saw a lot. A growing number of black people were earning a good living. McWilliams met black doctors, lawyers, and business owners. They were well educated, well dressed, and sophisticated. She admired their fine clothes and dignified manners.

In 1904 an international exposition, or gigantic fair, was held in St. Louis. It lasted almost a year, and more than 19 million people were dazzled by hundreds of exhibits. There were displays of hot-air balloons, automobiles, and a huge clock decorated with millions of flowers. The first ice-cream cones were sold by a vendor who rolled up a waffle and added a scoop of ice cream on top.

Fairgoers also heard speeches by famous people including Booker T. Washington, a prominent black educator. He had founded Tuskegee Institute, a school in Alabama that trained black students for industrial jobs. In 1901, Washington had also founded the National Negro Business League (NNBL), an organization of black businessmen.

Margaret Murray Washington, Washington's wife and herself a lecturer, teacher, and journalist, came to St. Louis, too. A leader of the National Association of Colored Women (NACW), Margaret Washington spoke to its St. Louis branch. McWil-

*Booker T. Washington, shown here on his horse, was
a black leader in business and education. After McWilliams
had changed her name to Walker, she met Washington.
At first, he ignored her. Eventually, however, he invited
her to speak at an NNBL convention.*

liams heard her and was captivated by her elegant appearance and confident words. She listened carefully as Washington explained that the aim of NACW was the "development of its women, mentally, morally and industrially . . . and [its] motto is, 'Lifting as we climb.'"

McWilliams was determined to lift herself up, but she did not know how. "I was considered a good washerwoman and laundress. I am proud of that fact," she later said, "but, work as I would, I seldom could make more than $1.50 a day." She thought about her situation a lot. One time, she said, "As I bent over the washboard, and looked at my arms buried in soap suds, I said to myself, 'What are you going to do when you grow old and your back gets stiff?' But with all my thinking, I couldn't see how I, a poor washerwoman, was going to better my condition."

While McWilliams was thinking about how to improve her life, she was also worrying about her hair. No matter what she did, her hair remained brittle and broken, and it was falling out in spots. She tried various hair products, including Wonderful Hair Grower made by Poro Company. Founded by Annie N. Turnbo Malone in 1900, Poro Company was located near St. Louis, and sometimes McWilliams worked as an agent selling Poro products door to door.

There are at least two explanations for what happened next. Some people believe that McWilliams analyzed the hair product that she used, copied the formula, and added her own "secret" ingredient, which was probably sulfur. But, according to McWilliams, "He [God] answered my prayer, for one night I had a dream, and in that dream a big black man appeared to me and told me what to mix up for my hair. Some of the remedy was grown in Africa, but I sent for it, mixed it, put it on my scalp, and in a few weeks my hair was coming in faster than it had ever fallen out."

By about 1905, Sarah McWilliams realized that by solving her hair problem she had found a way to better her life. As she later explained, "I tried it on my friends; it helped them. I made up my mind to begin to sell it."

But first, instead of trying to compete with the Poro Company in St. Louis, McWilliams decided to move. This time she went to Denver, Colorado, the city where her brother Alex had moved. Although Alex had died, his wife and four daughters still lived there. McWilliams arrived on July 21, 1905. She was thirty-seven years old. The city of Denver was only ten years older than she.

Founded in 1858 after prospectors found gold at Cherry Creek, Denver was booming. Silver had been discovered in the nearby Rocky Mountains. Railroad tracks connected Denver to every major city in the United States. Miners and ranchers crowded the streets. Ten miles to the west towered the mighty Rockies with their year-round cover of snow.

At one mile high, Denver's thin air made McWilliams short of breath at first. But, determined to start her new business, she adjusted fast. "There is no royal flower strewn road to success," she said, "and if there is I have not found it, for what success I have attained is the result of many sleepless nights and hard work."

McWilliams rented a room in an attic, where she perfected her formula. Night after night she experimented by mixing different ingredients in her washtub. During the day, she washed clothes. She was also a cook, probably at a lunch counter in a drugstore. Within months, McWilliams developed three products that worked beautifully on her hair and her nieces'—Wonderful Hair Grower, Glossine, and Vegetable Shampoo. She also redesigned a steel comb with wider gaps between the teeth to use with the thicker hair that black people usually have.

Carefully groomed and usually dressed in a white blouse and a long, dark skirt, McWilliams started selling her products door to door. She always gave a free demonstration by washing the customer's hair with the Vegetable Shampoo. Then she put Wonderful Hair Grower on the customer's hair and scalp to control dandruff and other scalp problems. Next she applied the Glossine, or light oil, to soften the hair and pressed it with a steel comb that she had heated on the stove. By using the oil and hot comb, McWilliams straightened out the tight curls that most of her black customers had and left their hair shiny and smooth. She eventually called her approach the Walker Hair Care Method.

A box of Walker's first product: Wonderful Hair Grower. The picture on the box shows her after she used the product.

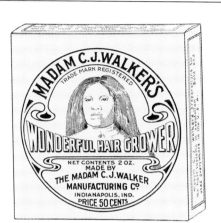

Before long, she developed a full line of products.

23

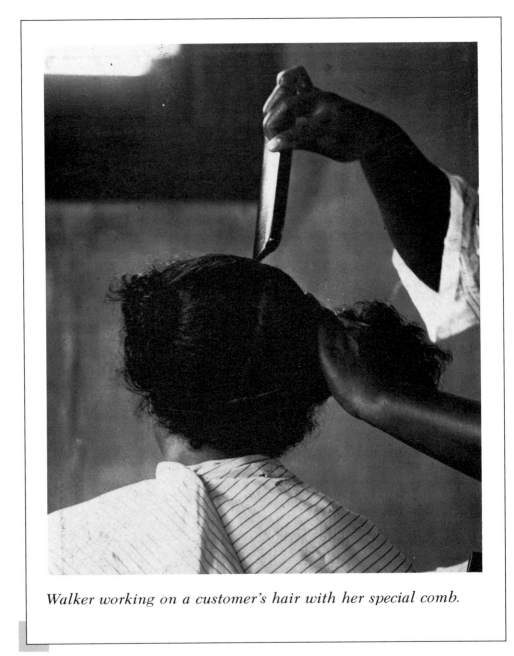

Walker working on a customer's hair with her special comb.

McWilliams was not shy about telling customers how her products had dramatically improved her appearance. She used before and after pictures of herself in advertisements and on her products. People ordered her products through the mail.

She wrote letters about her successes to Charles Joseph Walker, who had become her close friend and adviser when she lived in St. Louis. Walker, a newspaperman known as C. J., responded with encouragement, and he gave her advice about advertising and promotion. Soon he came to Denver, and on January 4, 1906, he and McWilliams were married. From then on, McWilliams used the name Madam C. J. Walker, a name that she thought sounded dignified.

C. J. Walker was satisfied when Madam's business started earning $10 a day, and he thought she should be, too. But she was not. According to Madam, "I was convinced that my hair preparations would fill a long-felt want, and when we found it impossible to agree, due to his narrowness of vision, I embarked in business for myself."

In September 1906, Madam Walker left on a sales trip. She was gone for eighteen months and traveled by train to nine states. Lelia, who had graduated from college, moved to Denver to handle the business her mother was generating. Women in states as far apart as Oklahoma and New York were ordering products from Walker. She sent the orders to Denver, where Lelia and her cousins Anjetta, Thrisapen, Mattie, and Gladis mailed the products to the customers. Madam was also recruiting and training women to be sales agents for Walker products.

In 1908, Walker decided to move again. This time she picked the thriving city of Pittsburgh, Pennsylvania. During her travels, Walker had visited Pittsburgh and recognized the business potential. An increasing number of black people were beginning to prosper there. And Pittsburgh was much closer than Denver to major cities with large black populations, such as New York, Washington, D.C., and Baltimore.

Madam Walker and Lelia arrived in Pittsburgh in the summer of 1908 and opened a beauty parlor. They also founded Lelia College, a school for training Walker agents, whom Walker began to call "hair culturists." Lelia College also offered a $25 correspondence course in the Walker Hair Care Method.

Most black women worked very hard for little money and, with few exceptions, were limited to being maids, washerwomen, and farm workers. Madam Walker offered them a way to be their own boss and earn more money. "I am endeavoring to provide employment for hundreds of the women of my race," Walker said. Hundreds, and later thousands, of black women jumped at the chance. Walker was very proud that she had "made it possible for many colored women to abandon the washtub for more pleasant and profitable occupations."

Two years later, in 1910, Madam moved again. This time she went to Indianapolis, Indiana, the capital and largest city in the state. George L. Knox, a successful black newspaper owner, persuaded Walker to move there because Indianapolis, a major hub for railroad transportation in America, also had a thriving black community.

W*alker and* her husband settled in Indianapolis in the spring of 1910. Lelia, who had married John

Robinson, stayed in Pittsburgh to run Walker's business. Walker established a beauty school, a laboratory, and a factory where her products were developed and made. Knox introduced her to Robert Lee Brokenburr, a young black lawyer. In September 1911, Brokenburr filed the necessary papers to legally establish the Madam C. J. Walker Manufacturing Company with Madam Walker as the sole stockholder. Brokenburr also became assistant manager for the company.

Another young black lawyer, Freeman Briley Ransom, known as F. B. Ransom, agreed to manage Walker's business. Walker hired many black women, including Violet Davis Reynolds, Walker's private secretary; Alice Kelly, the factory forewoman and the only other person except for Madam and Lelia who knew the secret formula; and Marjorie Joyner, the national supervisor of Walker's chain of beauty schools and the inventor of a permanent waving machine. Walker also hired her sister Louvenia (long since divorced) as a worker in the Indianapolis factory and her nieces Thrisapen and Anjetta Breedlove as Walker agents in Los Angeles.

A photograph of Walker taken in 1910, the year she moved to Indianapolis, Indiana.

Walker on the steps of her house, where she opened a beauty salon, laboratory, and factory. The sign between the second floor windows reads: Madam C. J. Walker Hair Culturist 640 N. West St.

A Walker Company delivery truck loaded with Walker products.

Walker's business expanded rapidly. She added new products to her list, including Temple Grower ("To force short, unsightly hairs on the temple, neck and forehead to respond to growth") and Tetter Salve ("Combats disease and insures healthy scalps and improved hair"). Walker also signed up new agents to sell her products and opened more beauty schools.

As Walker's Hair Care Method became more popular, it also became controversial. Some black people accused Walker of straightening black women's hair to make it look like white women's hair. Black ministers said that if black people were supposed to have straight hair then God would have given it to them.

"Let me correct the erroneous impression held by some that I claim to straighten hair," Madam Walker replied. "I deplore such an impression because I have always held myself out as a hair culturist." True, Walker's method straightened black women's hair, but, according to Walker, her purpose was to help women have healthy hair and scalps. Walker also stressed the importance of cleanliness and personal hygiene. One of her advertisements read, "The Key to Beauty, Success and Happiness is a good appearance."

In 1912, George Knox told Walker about the National Negro Business League (NNBL) convention in Chicago. He was going, and he thought the members should hear about her success. Walker agreed to join him in Chicago. But during the convention, Booker T. Washington, the president, ignored Knox's efforts to introduce Walker. Finally, Walker jumped to her feet and addressed Washington herself:

Surely you are not going to shut the door in my face. I feel that I am in a business that is a credit to the womanhood of our race. . . . I am a woman who came from the cotton fields of the South. I was promoted from there to the washtub. Then I was promoted to the cook kitchen, and from there I promoted myself into the business of manufacturing hair goods and preparations. I have built my own factory on my own ground.

Washington never ignored Walker again. In fact, he invited her to speak at the next NNBL Convention.

hat same year, Walker divorced C. J. Walker. She also became a grandmother when A'Lelia (Lelia had added the *A*'), who had also divorced her husband, adopted Mae Bryant. Walker loved her new granddaughter. Mae, who had long, thick hair, sometimes traveled with Walker and modeled her products.

Walker worked hard selling products, recruiting agents, and promoting her business. She traveled almost constantly—to Seattle, Minneapolis, Portland, Houston, Charleston, and Los Angeles and as far as Jamaica, Cuba, and Panama. Although there were telephones at the time, they were not as easy to find or use as they are today, and telegrams were not practical for long messages. So, Walker and Ransom kept in touch by sending each other a steady stream of letters.

Back and forth Walker and Ransom wrote about business matters. "What is the trouble that the people [her agents] can not get their orders?" Walker wrote in one letter. "People jump on me as if I was there [in Indianapolis] looking after the things and of course I get all the blame. Now I don't know who is to blame but these conditions must be eliminated." In another letter she wrote, "Yes, I say it is remarkable the way my bank account continues to increase and also remarkable how I continue to draw on it. While this has been the most expensive trip I have ever taken in America, I feel, however, that the returns will full[y] compensate."

Walker surrounded herself with well-educated people and asked them questions about anything she did not know. She kept working on her reading and writing. An articulate, outspoken woman, Walker loved to discuss politics. Her friends included such outstanding black intellectuals and civil rights activists as Mary McLeod Bethune and W.E.B. Du Bois.

In 1913, A'Lelia opened a beauty salon in New York City. It was located in a town house Walker bought in a section of the city known as Harlem. Three years later, Madam Walker moved there to live with A'Lelia and Mae.

Harlem was an exciting place to be. A huge migration of black people from the rural South to the cities of the North had just begun and would continue throughout the 1920s. This shift in popula-

THE MME. C. J. WALKER
MANUFACTURING CO.
HEADQUARTERS AND FACTORY
640 NORTH WEST STREET
INDIANAPOLIS, IND.

NEW PHONE, 26-117
OLD MAIN, 7256

MANUFACTURERS OF
MME. WALKER'S
WONDERFUL HAIR GROWER

Lelia
College
for
Treating and Teaching
Mme. Walker's
method of
Hair
Growing

BRANCH OFFICES
NEW YORK CITY
2303 SEVENTH AVENUE
COR. 135TH STREET

BROOKLYN
782 FULTON STREET

LELIA COLLEGE
108-110 WEST 136TH STREET
NEW YORK CITY

St. Louis Mo.
Mar. 6, 1918

My dear Mr. Ransom,
I am writing
to say that I have lost the
address of the gary lady. I also
want Mrs. Shoy, Sims' address
Please send them immediately
If you have to wire them to me.
Please tell me at what churches I am
will speak. Yours Truly
Mme. C. J. Walker.

During her extensive travels, Walker wrote many
letters to the manager of her company, F. B. Ransom.
Sometimes she wrote on plain paper. For this letter
she used her formal business stationery.

tion was called the Great Migration. Harlem, which drew the largest number of people, became known as the Negro Mecca. Black poets, writers, artists, and musicians were settling there. Businesses owned by black people were thriving. "There is so much more joy living in New York," Walker exclaimed in a letter to Ransom.

That same year Walker organized her agents into local groups called The Madam C. J. Walker Hair Culturists Union of America. "We organized mainly for the protection of the agents and to keep others from infringing on the prices [by] selling the goods under price," she wrote to Ransom. Agents attended local meetings and national conventions. They received awards for community work.

Madam C. J. Walker became very rich and very famous. She continued to promote her business, but she also enjoyed the money it had brought her. She loved cars, clothes, jewelry, and giving elegant parties. She loved music and bought a gold-leaved grand piano and harp, a ceiling-high organ, and a state-of-the-art Victrola, or phonograph.

Walker loved automobiles. In this photograph, taken about 1912 in Indianapolis, Indiana, she sits at the steering wheel. Beside her is Anjetta Breedlove, her niece. Directly behind Walker is Linda Flint, her secretary, and Alice Kelly, forewoman of Walker's factory, sits beside Flint.

In this picture, Walker is at the wheel of her electric car.

Walker also shared some of the money she made. She became a philanthropist—one of the few black people at the time who were wealthy enough to donate huge sums of money to causes, organizations, and people. She gave thousands of dollars to Mary McLeod Bethune to help her with the school she had started in Florida. She gave money to the National Association for the Advancement of Colored People (NAACP), an organization founded in 1909 to "promote equality of rights and eradicate race prejudice among the citizens of the United States." Walker's money was behind many black artists and writers who were struggling to produce their works during the beginning of the exciting period called the Harlem Renaissance. She also contributed to churches, cultural centers, and YMCAs.

Walker also worked hard to end discrimination against black people. Between 1917 and 1919 there were several hundred riots directed against blacks in northern cities, mostly in the Midwest. In 1917 Walker was part of a group that went to Washington, D.C., to try to persuade President Woodrow Wilson and Congress to make lynching and mob

Walker donated money to restore the Washington, D.C., home of the famous black leader, Frederick Douglass. Today visitors to Douglass's home can see this plaque in honor of Walker's generosity.

Walker's friend Mary McLeod Bethune founded a school for young black women that became Bethune-Cookman College. Walker's picture hangs in the oval frame above Bethune.

violence a federal crime. That same year Walker agents sent a telegram from their national convention to Wilson to "protest against the continuation of such wrongs and injustice in this land of the free and home of the brave."

In 1918 Walker moved again. She had built a spectacular thirty-room mansion on a four-and-a-half-acre estate high above the Hudson River in Irvington-on-Hudson. Irvington, not far from New York City, was a small town of mostly wealthy white people.

Called Villa Lewaro (Lewaro was from the first two letters of each part of her daughter's name, *Le*lia *Wa*lker *Ro*binson), Walker's mansion was designed by the black architect Vertner Woodson Tandy. Walker lived there with A'Lelia and Mae. She loved to entertain, and Villa Lewaro was the scene of many parties.

Madam Walker dressed elegantly. A reporter who interviewed her at her villa wrote that "When she came into the room [Walker] carried her generous weight gracefully on high French heels and wore an expensive pink-flowered lavender silk dressing gown."

Walker held many parties and meetings at Villa Lewaro.
Posed in front of her mansion (top) is a group of Walker agents.
In this photo of the back of the mansion (below), agents line up
on Lewaro's many patios and by its graceful fountain.

For several years, Ransom had asked Walker to rest. She had high blood pressure, and he worried about her health. But Madam C. J. Walker would not slow down.

Finally, during a trip to St. Louis in 1919, Walker became so ill that she was rushed home in a private railroad car. At Villa Lewaro, her doctor told her that her condition was grave. Ransom arrived from Indianapolis, and Walker gave him instructions, including a list of organizations to help with gifts of money.

One day in May 1919, Walker's nurse heard her say, "I want to live to help my race." Those were her last words. She went into a coma, and, on May 25, 1919, Madam C. J. Walker died. She was fifty-one years old.

After a funeral at Villa Lewaro, Madam C. J. Walker was buried in Woodlawn Cemetery in New York City. Scores of people and organizations honored Walker's memory with glowing words. But of all the spoken and written tributes, Madam C. J. Walker's own words describe her best: "Perseverance is my motto."

Madam C. J. Walker's headstone in Woodlawn Cemetery in New York City. Her daughter, A'Lelia, who died suddenly at the age of 46, is buried beside Walker.

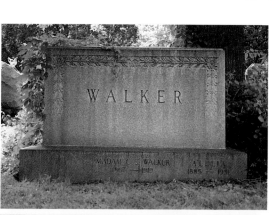

After Walker's death, F. B. Ransom continued as general manager of her company. In 1936, he attended a graduation ceremony for a group of Walker hair culturists in Chicago, Illinois. Ransom is seated in the front row.

Important Dates

1867 Sarah Breedlove, later known as Madam C. J. Walker, is born in Delta, Louisiana, on December 23.

1874 Breedlove's parents are stricken with yellow fever and die.

1878 Breedlove and her sister Louvenia move to Vicksburg, Mississippi.

1882 Breedlove marries Moses (Jeff) McWilliams.

1887 Jeff McWilliams dies, and Sarah moves to St. Louis, Missouri, with her two-year-old daughter Lelia (later known as A'Lelia).

1905 Sarah McWilliams moves to Denver, Colorado, and starts building her business empire.

1906 McWilliams marries Charles Joseph Walker and becomes known as Madam C. J. Walker.

1908 Madam and Lelia move to Pittsburgh, Pennsylvania, where they open a beauty parlor and Lelia College, a school for training Walker agents.

1910 Madam moves to Indianapolis, Indiana, and establishes a beauty school, laboratory, and factory.

1916 Madam moves to New York City, where A'Lelia has opened a beauty salon three years before.

1917   The first Madam C. J. Walker Hair Culturists Union of America convention is held. Along with other prominent people, Walker goes to the White House to urge President Wilson to make lynching and mob violence a federal crime.

1918   Villa Lewaro is completed, and Madam moves into her mansion in Irvington-on-Hudson, New York.

1919   Madam C. J. Walker dies on May 25.

A post card from about 1922 showing headquarters of the Walker Manufacturing Company. A'Lelia had the building built in honor of her mother to "serve as the social and cultural center of the black community in Indianapolis." In addition to housing the Walker Company, the building was the site of a theater, casino, and coffee shop. Today the building is home to the Walker Urban Life Center.

Further Information

Books
Bundles, A'Lelia. *Madam C. J. Walker.* New York: Chelsea House, 1992.

McKissack, Patricia and Fredrick. *Madam C. J. Walker: Self-Made Millionaire.* Hillside, N.J.: Enslow Publishers, 1992.

Video
Madam C. J. Walker. Schlessinger Video Productions, Box 1110, Bala Cynwyd, PA, 19004; (215) 667-0200.

Places to Visit
The Graves of Madam C. J. Walker and her daughter A'Lelia, The Woodlawn Cemetery, Webster Avenue and 233rd Street, Bronx, New York.

Madame C. J. Walker Urban Life Center, 617 Indiana Avenue, Indianapolis, Indiana.

Villa Lewaro, North Broadway Avenue (also route U.S. 9), Irvington-on-Hudson, New York. At this time, Walker's mansion is not open to the public, but it is an impressive sight from the street, and plans are underway to open it as a museum.

Index